The WORDSWORTHS

By Mick Manning and Brita Granström

W
FRANKLIN WATTS
LONDON·SYDNEY

Welcome to Grasmere

Yet when I sit on rock or hill,
Down looking on the valley fair,
That Cottage with its clustering trees
Summons my heart; it settles there.
  From 'Grasmere – A Fragment' by Dorothy Wordsworth

The mountain paths around Grasmere can be steep so wait awhile to catch your breath. I will tell you the story of how my brother William and I set up home here, inspired one another and shared our lives. We found peace here, living simply and plainly, while our thoughts soared as high as the mountain ravens. We arrived at our new home, Dove Cottage in the Lake District, in 1799.

My Early Days

Much converse do I find in Thee,
Historian of my Infancy!
    From 'To a Butterfly' by William Wordsworth

Before I tell you about our life in Grasmere, let me tell you a little about the years that came before ... I was born in a little town on the edge of the Lake District and our parents were quite well-to-do. I had four brothers: Richard, John, Christopher and of course William, who became my dearest friend.

However, when I was only six years old, tragedy struck. Our poor mother died and our father, unable to cope, sent me away to live with an aunt.

The aunt lived in Halifax, a Yorkshire town with many factories. This was the age of the Industrial Revolution. Mechanical inventions, powered by steam and coal, revolutionised factories and mills but began to pollute the world.

Meanwhile, William and my other brothers were packed off to a boarding school in Hawkshead, in the heart of the Lake District.

"You may call me Dorothy."

Sadly our father died when I was 12, leaving the family rather poor. When I was about 15, I was sent to live with an uncle in Norfolk, where I helped teach girls at his Sunday School.

"This is my college."

"At last, we can begin a life together."

By this time William was a young man, studying at Cambridge University, not far from where I was living. This meant that we were able to meet up sometimes.

5

William's Schooldays

The Child is the father of the Man;
I could wish my days to be
Bound each to each by natural piety.
     From 'The Rainbow' by William Wordsworth

William was studying to be a lawyer but he wasn't interested in law as he really wanted to be a poet. On our walks together he told me about the schoolboy adventures he'd had while I was stuck in Halifax with our aunt. He had been encouraged, so he said with a smile, by 'Mother Nature', and he would one day write about these escapades. This is one of my favourites. William loved high speed skating games such as 'hare and hounds' and this next verse makes us feel the speed of the skaters ...

... All shod with steel,
We hissed along the polished ice in games
Confederate, imitative of the chase
And woodland pleasures, the resounding horn,
The pack loud chiming, and the hunted hare.
So through the darkness and the cold we flew,
And not a voice was idle; with the din,
   From *The Prelude* by William Wordsworth

..., and when the Vales
And woods were warm, was I a plunderer then
In the high places, on the lonesome peaks
Where'er, among the mountains and the winds,
The Mother Bird had built her lodge. Though mean
My object, and inglorious, yet the end
Was not ignoble. Oh! when I have hung
Above the raven's nest, by knots of grass
And half-inch fissures in the slippery rock
    From *The Prelude* by William Wordsworth

Raven's Eggs

Where'er, among the mountains and the winds,
The Mother Bird had built her lodge [...]
    From *The Prelude* by William Wordsworth

William told me another story about how he once climbed a cliff to steal ravens' eggs. It might seem wrong to you now, that as a nature-loving schoolboy, William stole birds' eggs. But wild birds had no laws protecting them then and were, often unfairly, seen as pests. William may have been paid by a farmer to take those beautiful speckled eggs, in the belief that fewer ravens would mean more new-born lambs surviving on the fells. I think William was very brave to climb up to that raven's nest, and I daresay he would have loved every minute of that dangerous adventure!

One evening (surely I was led by her)
I went alone into a Shepherd's Boat,
A Skiff that to a Willow tree was tied
Within a rocky Cave, its usual home. ...

I pushed, and struck the oars and struck again
In cadence, and my little Boat moved on
Even like a Man who walks with stately step
Though bent on speed. It was an act of stealth
And troubled pleasure; not without the voice
Of mountain-echoes did my Boat move on,
Leaving behind her still on either side
Small circles glittering idly in the moon,
Until they melted all into one track
Of sparkling light. ...

When from behind that craggy Steep, till then
The bound of the horizon, a huge Cliff,
As if with voluntary power instinct,
Upreared its head. I struck, and struck again
And, growing still in stature, the huge Cliff
Rose up between me and the stars, and still,
With measured motion, like a living thing,
Strode after me. With trembling hands I turned,
And through the silent water stole my way
Back to the Cavern of the Willow tree. ...

But huge and mighty Forms that do not live
Like living men moved slowly through the mind
By day and were the trouble of my dreams.
       From *The Prelude* by William Wordsworth

A Mountain Giant

And, growing still in stature, the huge Cliff
Rose up between me and the stars, and still,
With measured motion, like a living thing,
Strode after me. ...
　　From *The Prelude* by William Wordsworth

William also confessed to me that he had once 'borrowed' a rowing boat (he claimed 'Mother Nature' led him astray). Anyway, he rowed the boat out in the darkness, across a deep lake called Ullswater. Then, as he was rowing, a mountain seemed to loom over the horizon like an angry giant! Full of guilt he took the boat back to where he had untied it. Poor William, he had nightmares about that 'giant' for weeks. One day this, and the other adventures, would become some of the most memorable parts of his wonderful poem *The Prelude*.

Together at Last

'The Giant Wordsworth – God love him!'
Samuel Taylor Coleridge

We met up when we could but we were too poor to do what we wanted, which was to share a house together. Then in 1795 a friend of William's died, leaving William money in his will. At last William could be independent and be a poet. We rented a house in Dorset for two years and then, in 1797, moved to Somerset, to a house close to our new poet friend, Samuel Taylor Coleridge and his wife Sara. William and Coleridge began to write poetry together, poems that used everyday language about everyday people. In 1798 they published *Lyrical Ballads*.

Let's publish together!

We'll call it Lyrical Ballads.

Although it got terrible reviews at first, *Lyrical Ballads* would eventually inspire a new movement, later named Romanticism.

We were so poor that we often had to beg our new friends for their old clothes but we didn't care. We were free!

Our noisy parties at all times of the day or night led to us being accused of being French spies by some of the local people!

Inspired by a Welsh walking holiday together, William composed a beautiful poem for me called 'Lines Written a Few Miles above Tintern Abbey'. These lines come towards the end:

> For thou art with me, here, upon the banks
> Of this fair river; thou, my dearest Friend,
> My dear, dear Friend; and in thy voice I catch
> The language of my former heart, and read
> My former pleasures in the shooting lights
> Of thy wild eyes. Oh! yet a little while
> May I behold in thee what I was once,
> My dear, dear Sister! ...

Our Own Cottage, 1799

The naked trees,
The icy brooks, as on we passed, appeared
To question us. 'Whence come ye? To what end?'
They seemed to say, 'What would ye,' said the shower,
'Wild Wanderers, whither through my dark domain?'
The Sunbeam said, 'Be happy.'
    From 'Home at Grasmere' by William Wordsworth

Then, one day, during a walking holiday in our beloved Lake District, William discovered a cottage to rent. In his poem 'Home at Grasmere', William suggested the powers of nature had guided his steps. I had to agree as it was the most charming cottage I had ever seen, nestling as it did at the foot of the wild mountain landscape. We moved in just before Christmas 1799 and I wrote a poem describing it as 'the very Mountains' child.'

Behold Dorothy, our future home together!

It is like the mountain's child nestling there!

When I opened the door it was cold and damp, but it was my cold! And my damp! It was beautiful to me and I couldn't wait to move in ...

We needed to turn those cold, empty rooms into a home. I paid a sweep to clean the chimneys because they smoked so badly and I got to work ...

Home at Grasmere

*−I love that house because it is
The very Mountains' child.*
  From 'Grasmere – A Fragment' by Dorothy Wordsworth

I swept, scrubbed, dusted and polished and that cottage soon felt like home. I sewed new, draught-proof curtains for the windows and four-poster beds and there seemed no end of work to do. But I did join William outdoors when I could. I remember one evening especially: it was crisp and frosty and together we walked up the road a little way. We stood and gazed across the lake at the mountains silhouetted against the night sky until the icy cold gave me toothache.

It was mid-winter and getting washed was so cold! There was no bathroom, only an outside toilet!

...Where'er my footsteps turned,
Her Voice was like a hidden Bird that sang;
The thought of her was like a flash of light
Or an unseen companionship, a breath
Of fragrance independent of the wind;
From 'Home at Grasmere' by
William Wordsworth

My Journal Begins...

There was a roaring in the wind all night;
The rain came heavily and fell in floods;
But now the sun is rising calm and bright;
The birds are singing in the distant woods
   From 'Resolution and Independence'
by William Wordsworth

I didn't begin my Grasmere Journal until May, 1800. Before that we had so much to do. But when William and John departed for a three-week visit to our old friend Mary Hutchinson's home, I realised (despite my tears) that I could use the lonely weeks that stretched ahead to begin my journal. William should have something of mine to read when he returned to me!

Farewell dear sister...

Wednesday, 14th May, 1800
William and John set off into Yorkshire after dinner at half-past two o'clock, cold pork in their pockets. I left them at the turning of the Low Wood bay ... I sat a long time upon a stone at the margin of the lake, and after a flood of tears my heart was easier.

Friday, 16th May, 1800
Grasmere was very solemn in the last glimpse of twilight. It calls home the heart to quietness. I had been very melancholy in my walk back. I had many of my saddest thoughts, and I could not keep the tears within me.

Thrush

Stonechat

Tuesday Morning, 20th May, 1800
Everything green and overflowing with life, and the streams making a perpetual song, with the thrushes, and all little birds, not forgetting the stone-chats...

14th May (continued)
At Rydale, a woman of the village, stout and well-dressed, begged a half-penny. She had never she said done it before, but these hard times!

... The postman was not come in — I walked as far as Windermere, and met him there.

This is the Spot

*We two have had such happy hours together
That my heart melts in me to think of it.*
   From 'Travelling' by William Wordsworth

I had always chosen prose for my journals. Prose was my way to record our life together: the nature walks, hard work in the garden; country folk and the homeless people we met, and of course my moods and feelings about all of it. Here are some more extracts ...

William will enjoy reading this when he returns ...

William will enjoy these flowers ...

Monday, 2nd June, 1800
A cold dry windy morning. I worked in the garden, and planted flowers etc ... sat under the trees after dinner until tea time.

I went to Ambleside after tea, crossed the stepping-stones at the foot of Grasmere, and pursued my way on the other side of Rydale and by Clappersgate.

2nd June (continued)
I sat a long time to watch the hurrying waves, and to hear the regularly irregular sound of the dashing waters. The waves round about the little Island seemed like a dance of spirits that rose out of the water, round its small circumference of shore.

I've missed you so …

Saturday, 7th June, 1800
I heard a foot go to the front of the house, turn round, and open the gate. It was William! After our first joy was over, we got some tea. We did not go to bed till 4 o'clock in the morning, so he had an opportunity of seeing our improvements.

This is the spot:—how mildly does the sun
Shine in between the fading leaves! the air
In the habitual silence of this wood
Is more than silent: and this bed of heath,
Where shall we find so sweet a resting-place?
Come!—let me see thee sink into a dream
Of quiet thoughts,—protracted till thine eye
Be calm as water when the winds are gone
And no one can tell whither.—my sweet friend!
We two have had such happy hours together
That my heart melts in me to think of it.
From 'Travelling' by William Wordsworth

"Here's some bread for you both."

Tuesday, 27th May, 1800
A very tall woman, tall much beyond the measure of tall women, called at the door. She had on a very long brown cloak, and a very white cap, without bonnet. Her face was excessively brown, but it had plainly once been fair.

The Beggars

She gave me eyes, she gave me ears,
And humble cares, and delicate fears;
  From 'The Sparrow's Nest' by William Wordsworth

Coleridge put it so well when he once said prose was 'words in their best order' and poetry 'the best words in the best order'. Prose was my 'voice' and poetry was William's and so I was always delighted when the prose of my journals inspired his poems. Yet sometimes, he struggled to find better words than I had already written. My journal entry about a beautiful beggar woman, written when he was away, had just that effect when I read it to him later. He began to write his own poetic version but grew so frustrated that he left the poem unfinished and retired exhausted to bed.

Afterwards on my way to Ambleside, beside the bridge at Rydale, I saw her husband sitting by the roadside, his two asses feeding beside him ...

27th May (continued)
I passed on and about a quarter of a mile further I saw two boys before me, one about ten, the other eight years old, at play chasing a butterfly. They were wild figures, not very ragged, but without shoes and stockings; the hat of the elder was wreathed round with yellow flowers, the younger whose hat was only a rimless crown, had stuck it round with laurel leaves.

What a charming sight!

But William didn't give up and, after a good night's sleep, woke early and finished his poem the 'Beggars' before our breakfast.

She had a tall Man's height, or more;
No bonnet screened her from the heat;
A long drab-coloured Cloak she wore,
A Mantle reaching to her feet:
What other dress she had I could not know;
Only she wore a Cap that was as white as snow.
I left her, and pursued my way;
And soon before me did espy
A pair of little Boys at play,
Chasing a crimson butterfly;
The Taller followed with his hat in hand,
Wreathed round with yellow flow'rs, the gayest of the land.
   From 'Beggars' by William Wordsworth

Our Garden

O happy Garden! whose seclusion deep
Hath been so friendly to industrious hours;
  From 'A Farewell' by
William Wordsworth

We lived plainly but we grew a lot of our own vegetables. In fact we loved gardening. I had planted beautiful (and tasty) scarlet runner beans against the house and there were fruit trees to prune and harvest in the orchard.

Monday 19 May, 1800
Sauntered a good deal in the garden, bound carpets, mended old clothes, read Timon of Athens, dried linen ...

Monday, 9th June, 1800
In the morning William cut down the winter cherry tree. I sowed French beans and weeded.

Wednesday, 11th June, 1800
I sowed kidney-beans and spinach, a cold evening. Molly stuck the peas. I weeded a little. Did not walk.

Monday, 4th August, 1800
I tied up scarlet beans, nailed the honeysuckles, etc. etc.

4th August (continued)
I pulled a large basket of peas...

Sunday, 12th October, 1800
We pulled apples after dinner,
a large basket full.

Pike Fishing

Our boat is safely anchored by the shore,
And there will safely ride when we are gone;
The flowering shrubs that deck our humble door
Will prosper, though untended and alone:
    From 'A Farewell' by William Wordsworth

We didn't just eat vegetables. I baked and made soup. We bought meat from the butcher and we fished in the lake in our own rowing boat. We often caught pike. They were large, fierce fish so it was quite a thrill to catch them. They were tasty, once cooked, but very, very boney!

Thursday, 29th May, 1800
Miss Simpson, and Miss Falcon, and Mr S. came very early. Went to Mr. Gell's boat before tea. We fished upon the lake and amongst us caught 13 Bass.

Thursday, 12th June, 1800
William and I went upon the water to set pike floats. John fished under Loughrigg. We returned to dinner, two pikes boiled and roasted.

Friday, 14th June, 1800
A rainy morning. William and John went upon the lake. Very warm and pleasant, gleams of sunshine. Went upon the water after tea, caught a pike 7 1/2 lbs. Mr. Simpson trolling.

15th October, 1801
William and I walked up Loughrigg Fell, then by the waterside. I held my head under a spout.

20th October, 1801
We went to the Langdales a very fine day.

Sunday, 25th October, 1801
Went upon Helvellyn. Glorious sights. The sea at Cartmel. The Scotch mountains beyond the sea to the right. Whiteside large, and round, and very soft, and green, behind us. Mists above and below, and close to us, with the sun amongst them.

Mountain Climbing

She loves her fire, her cottage-home;
Yet o'er the moorland will she roam
    From 'Louisa' by William Wordsworth

We hiked up many of the steep mountain paths together to see the breathtaking views for which the Lake District is so famous. We were as sure-footed as the mountain sheep; in fact William's poem 'Louisa' was inspired by me. Few women scrambled up the fells back then, but I did. I loved the sense of freedom and the wind in my face. In fact, many years later in 1818, I became the first woman to climb up England's highest peak, Scafell Pike, and write a letter at the top!

She loves her fire, her cottage-home;
Yet o'er the moorland will she roam
In weather rough and bleak;
And, when against the wind she strains,
Oh! might I kiss the mountain rains
That sparkle on her cheek.

Take all that's mine 'beneath the moon,'
If I with her but half a noon
May sit beneath the walls
Of some old cave, or mossy nook,
When up she winds along the brook
To hunt the waterfalls.
Verses 3 and 4 from 'Louisa' by William Wordsworth

Owl Hoots

There was a light of most strange birth,
A light that came out of the earth,
And spread along the dark hill-side.
    From 'Grasmere – A Fragment' by Dorothy Wordsworth

William and I would often walk down to the lakeside together on fine nights. William had been shown by a friend how to mimic the hoots of owls by blowing through cupped hands and it had already inspired his lovely poem 'There was a Boy'. We would hoot then sit and listen as the owls hooted back with quivering voices, so delicious in the darkness.

Wednesday, 17th March, 1802
The owls hooted when we sat on the wall at the foot of White Moss; the sky broke more and more, and we saw the moon now and then. John Green passed us with his cart ...

There were huge slow-travelling Clouds in the sky, that threw large masses of shade upon some of the mountains.

There was a Boy; ye know him well, ye cliffs
And islands of Winander! many a time,
At evening, when the earliest stars began
To move along the edges of the hills,
Rising or setting, would he stand alone,
Beneath the trees, or by the glimmering lake;
And there, with fingers interwoven, both hands
Pressed closely palm to palm and to his mouth
Uplifted, he, as through an instrument,
Blew mimic hootings to the silent owls
That they might answer him.—And they would shout
Across the watery vale, and shout again,
Responsive to his call,—with quivering peals,
And long halloos, and screams, and echoes loud
Redoubled and redoubled, ...
   From 'There was a Boy' by William Wordsworth

Thursday, 15th April, 1802
... I never saw daffodils so beautiful. They grew about the mossy stones about and about them, some rested their heads upon these stones as on a pillow for weariness and the rest tossed and reeled and danced and seemed as if they verily laughed with the wind that blew upon them over the lake.

Daffodils at Ullswater

When all at once I saw a crowd,
A host of golden Daffodils;
   From 'I Wandered Lonely as a Cloud'
by William Wordsworth

We would go out in all weathers! I'll never forget the windy April day when we came upon a mass of wild daffodils and had such fun thinking up ways to describe their beauty. I wrote about them in my journal and later William wrote what was to become his most famous poem, 'I Wandered Lonely as a Cloud'. And even though he wrote it as if he had been alone that day, rather than chattering with me, his poem captures perfectly those moments of wonder we shared.

I wandered lonely as a Cloud
That floats on high o'er Vales and Hills,
When all at once I saw a crowd,
A host, of golden daffodils;
Beside the Lake, beneath the trees,
Fluttering and dancing in the breeze.

Continuous as the stars that shine
And twinkle on the milky way,
They stretched in never-ending line
Along the margin of a bay:
Ten thousand saw I at a glance,
Tossing their heads in sprightly dance.
    Verses 1 and 2 from 'I Wondered Lonely as a Cloud' by William Wordsworth

William's Wedding

I slept a good deal of the night, and rose fresh and well in the morning. At a little after eight o'clock, I saw them go down the avenue towards the church.
From *Grasmere Journal* by Dorothy Wordsworth

In October 1802, my dear brother married our friend Mary Hutchinson. (Surely you had suspected all those visits to-and-fro had a purpose?) Before the wedding, he and I went on holiday to France together and on the way we were both deeply moved by the beauty of London in the early morning. That sight earned a place in my journal and inspired William to write one of his most famous poems, 'Composed upon Westminster Bridge'.

31st July, 1802
It was a beautiful morning. The City, St Pauls, with the River a multitude of little Boats, made a most beautiful sight as we crossed Westminster Bridge. The houses were not overhung by their cloud of smoke they were spread out endlessly ...

Earth has not any thing to show more fair:
Dull would he be of soul who could pass by
A sight so touching in its majesty:
This City now doth, like a garment, wear
The beauty of the morning; silent, bare,
Ships, towers, domes, theatres, and temples lie
Open unto the fields, and to the sky;
All bright and glittering in the smokeless air.
    First half of 'Composed upon Westminster Bridge, September 3, 1802' by William Wordsworth

The night before the wedding, held at Mary's family's church, William let me wear the wedding ring he was to give Mary ~ it was his promise that Mary would fit into our life together.

Despite Mary being a loving friend to me, I became distraught with worry that things wouldn't be the same when we got back to Grasmere.

"They are like such dear sisters!"

"The three of us shall have such fun together, Dorothy!"

William's promise came true and our merry band was reunited. William and Mary, our brother John, when he wasn't at sea, myself and Mary's sister Sara, all lived in Dove Cottage.

35

Late Night Poetry

Our great friend Coleridge, who was now living in Keswick with his family, thought nothing of striding out alone to join us. He often arrived so late he got us out of bed. Then he and William would read out their latest poems while we listened.

That sent shivers up my spine!

"What a poem!"

That sunny dome! those caves of ice!
And all who heard should see them there,
And all should cry, Beware! Beware!
His flashing eyes, his floating hair!
Weave a circle round him thrice,
And close your eyes with holy dread
For he on honey-dew hath fed,
And drunk the milk of Paradise.
   From 'Kubla Khan' by
Samuel Taylor Coleridge

Leaving Dove Cottage

FAREWELL, thou little Nook of mountain-ground,
   From 'A Farewell' by William Wordsworth

I became an aunt in 1803 when William and Mary's first child, baby John, was born. He was followed by little Dora in 1804 and baby Thomas in 1806. By 1808, when baby Catherine was born, we all sadly agreed we had outgrown our cottage and little garden. I shed copious tears the day we moved to a new home, Allen Bank in Grasmere.

Sweet garden-orchard, eminently fair,
The loveliest spot that man hath ever found,
Farewell!~~we leave thee to Heaven's peaceful care,
Thee, and the Cottage which thou dost surround.
   From 'A Farewell' by William Wordsworth

I love you Aunt Dorothy!

Is it too rainy to play outside today?

Allen Bank's chimneys smoked so badly we soon moved again; first to Grasmere parsonage and then, in 1812, as William started to receive gifts of money from Lord Lonsdale, we settled at Rydale Mount. Great sadness came to us that year as first little Catherine, then dear Thomas, died.

Rydal Mount

We settled into Rydal Mount, a fine house near Ambleside. We furnished it with fine carpets and beautiful furniture. Now we had servants and lots of space for the many guests who visited. William had a writing room and a library. When we designed the garden, we built a temple for plain living and high thinking: a stone hut. It was a sort of tribute to Dove Cottage, the home we once loved.

"I think you should invite Coleridge, William..."

By this time, William was seen as a hero by Romantic artists, such as the famous John Martin, who once gave him a signed print.

"My Dear Coleridge..."

By now William's poetry books, including *Lyrical Ballads* and *Poems in Two Volumes*, were recognised as truly great works.

41

The Hut

I had melancholy thoughts ...
a strangeness in my mind,
   From *The Prelude* by William Wordsworth

That simple hut, open to the fresh air but sheltered from the frequent Lake District showers, became William's true office and writing room in all but the coldest weather. Here he would 'escape' to be on his own to write and think and continue his life's work, a very long poem about how childhood can influence the person you become as an adult. (I already read bits of it to you at the beginning, about skating and ravens and stealing boats ...)
It was later called *The Prelude* and became a masterpiece of world literature, proving William to be Coleridge's 'Giant Wordsworth'.

The earth was all before me. With a heart
Joyous, nor scared at its own liberty,
I look about; and should the chosen guide
Be nothing better than a wandering cloud,
I cannot miss my way.
   From *The Prelude* by William Wordsworth

> Bleak season was it, turbulent and bleak,
> When hitherward we journeyed, side by side,
> Through bursts of sunshine and through flying showers.

43

Let Us Say Farewell

Farewell!--we leave thee to Heaven's peaceful care,
   From 'A Farewell' by William Wordsworth

But I must leave you now because the mist seems to be coming down and it's a long walk home. I have much to do: letters to write and the garden to tend. Let us say farewell and I'll leave you with some favourite lines from one of William's most bittersweet poems. It's about the passing of time, written during our earliest days in Grasmere, our days of plain living and high thinking.

There was a time when meadow, grove, and stream,
The earth, and every common sight,
To me did seem
Apparelled in celestial light,
The glory and the freshness of a dream.
It is not now as it hath been of yore;—
Turn wheresoe'er I may,
By night or day,
The things which I have seen I now can see no more.
    First verse from 'Ode: Intimations of Immortality from Recollections of Early Childhood'
by William Wordsworth

Afterword

William and Dorothy Wordsworth lived during a time of huge social and political change. As war raged in Europe against France, new inventions powered by steam and coal revolutionised mills and factories in England, making workers face unsafe and unhealthy conditions. Well-to-do women such as Dorothy Wordsworth were meant to marry and spend their time indoors, rather than walk for miles, write and go fishing. Dorothy's lifestyle was considered quite shocking in her day and it wasn't until years after her death that her writing was fully acknowledged.

William Wordsworth along with Coleridge inspired a movement known as the Romantics. It is now widely agreed that many of his greatest poems were written in or inspired by the years he lived in Dove Cottage. In 1843 William was offered the role of Poet Laureate. Although he turned the offer down at first he was persuaded eventually. He died at the age of 80 in 1850.

Dorothy Wordsworth is now recognised as being an important part of the Romantic movement in her own right. Her own delight in the landscape and people of the Lake District, captured in her journal writing, influenced her brother William's poetry. She also inspired several of William's most famous works. She died after a long illness in 1855.

Mary Wordsworth had been a childhood friend of both William and Dorothy. She often stayed at Dove Cottage, long before she and William married. Mary also wrote journals. She outlived both William and Dorothy, dying in 1859.

Samuel Taylor Coleridge was from Bristol but moved to the Lake District to live near the Wordsworths. He also travelled widely and lectured in London and was particularly knowledgable about William Shakespeare. He became addicted to opium and eventually left his family. He died in 1834. His best-known poems include 'Kubla Khan' and 'The Rime of the Ancient Mariner'.

The Romantics

As you may have already noticed in this book, the Romantic themes included nature, landscape, wild weather, medieval 'Gothic' ruins, legends and ghost stories. Both the Wordsworths and Samuel Taylor Coleridge are credited with influencing what was soon to become a massive European art movement. Other Romantics inlcude the authors Mary Shelley (*Frankenstein*) and Emily Brontë (*Wuthering Heights*) as well as painters such as J.M.W. Turner and Casper David Friedrich. Romantic composers include Ludvig van Beethoven and Fanny Mendelssohn.

First published in Great Britain in 2020 by The Watts Publishing Group

Text and illustrations © Mick Manning and Brita Granström 2020

The right of Mick Manning and Brita Granström to be identified as the authors and illustrators of this work have been asserted in accordance with the Copyright, Design and Patents Act, 1988.

Brita and Mick made the illustrations for this book based on studies they made while on location in the beautiful Lake District. Find out more at www.mickandbrita.com

Editor: Sarah Ridley and Paul Rockett
Design: Peter Scoulding after concept layouts by Mick and Brita
Cover design: Peter Scoulding

With thanks for the advice and expertise of The Wordsworth Trust, Dove Cottage and Wordsworth Museum staff.

A CIP catalogue record is available from the British Library.
HB ISBN: 978 1 4451 6862 3

Printed in China.

Franklin Watts
An imprint of Hachette Children's Group
Part of The Watts Publishing Group
Carmelite House, 50 Victoria Embankment, London EC4Y 0DZ

An Hachette UK Company

www.hachette.co.uk • www.franklinwatts.co.uk

For the Wordsworth Trust and the dedicated staff at Dove Cottage and the Wordsworth Museum

Mick and Brita used the following references and sources in the creation of this book: The Wordsworths' writings; especially Dorothy's *Grasmere Journal* and William's *Lyrical Ballads* and *The Prelude*. John Constable's tour of the Lake District 1806; images from the V&A Collection and the Wordsworth Trust Collection. Several week-long personal visits by the authors spent walking in the Wordsworths' footsteps and location drawing (while eating quite a lot of Grasmere gingerbread in the process). Mick and Brita and their publishers would like to thank The Wordsworth Trust and especially Catherine Kay (Education and Outreach Officer) for their kind support and an inspirational behind-the-scenes tour of Dove Cottage and the Wordsworth Museum.